Oxford Stage Company

in association with Royal and Derngate Theatres, Northampton
and Watford Palace Theatre

presents

PARADISE LOST

by John Milton

Adapted for the stage by Ben Power
Directed by Rupert Goold
Designed by Ben Stones
Lighting by Mark Jonathan
Music and sound by Adam Cork
Choreography by Liam Steel and Georgina Lamb
Video Design by Lorna Heavey

First performance of this production on 21 April 2006
at Watford Palace Theatre

D1166593

Cast

The Son	Charles Aitken
Moloch / Adam	Christian Bradley
Satan	Jasper Britton
Sin / Raphael	Caroline Faber
Beelzebub / Death / Gabriel	Stephen Fewell
Belial / Eve	Vinette Robinson

Creative Team

Adapter	Ben Power
Director	Rupert Goold
Designer	Ben Stones
Lighting Designer	Mark Jonathan
Composer & Sound Designer	Adam Cork
Choreography	Liam Steel & Georgina Lamb
Video Design	Lorna Heavey

For Paradise Lost

Production Manager	Patrick Molony
Company Stage Manager	Helen Reynolds
Deputy Stage Manager	Julia Reid
Technical Assistant Stage Manager	John Noe
Assistant Stage Manager	Val Cohen
Relighter / Production Electrician	Tom Snell
Costume Supervision	Kirsty Rowe & Jocelyn Creighton
Wardrobe Mistress	Louise Simpson
Production Carpenter	Mick Fernandez
Scenic Artists	Clare Jose, Aimee Bunyard & Frances Russell
Set transport	Paul Mathew
Lighting hires	White Light
Production Insurance	Walton & Parkinson
Press & Marketing	Julia Hallawell
Production Photography	Robert Day
Graphic Design	SWD

Production Acknowledgements:
Set built by Watford Palace Theatre Workshop and All Scene All Props;
Katie Bradford and Tina Kennedy; Darrel d'Silva, Jonjo O'Neill,
Leah Muller and Antony Bunsee; Nikki Amuka-Bird, Kate Fleetwood,
John McAndrew, David Tughan and Tim Pigott-Smith; Peter Eyre.

With special thanks to Ali Fellows

"You who bear witness…"
Paradise Lost from Poem to Play

When, in early 2003, Rupert Goold invited me to transform John Milton's ten-thousand line poem into a two-hour play, I was initially hesitant. The job of carving a living, contemporary piece of theatre out of the most famous and complex of English epics seemed an impossible one. I read and re-read the opening lines, and the rhythmic, alliterative power of the poetry (half-remembered from my time at university) was stunning. Surely there was no way these words could be placed in an actor's mouth? Surely the piece, as much philosophical investigation as poetic endeavour, only lived on paper, in the reader's mind? How could the lake of fire, the void of Chaos, the Garden of Eden, ever be realised on stage?

But then I was reminded that Milton had first envisaged the poem as a drama, a four-act tragedy, and I re-read it looking for evidence of its genesis as theatre. I was quickly struck by how much of the poem is dialogue, and by how much concerns character. Granted, its dialogue is of a style which at first seems complicated, labyrinthine, intellectual but undramatic. And yet, when trimmed, when rearranged, I began to see a dramatic essence which bore testament to Milton's original plan.

There are a number of key elements of the poem which, to me, feel theatrical. The structure is scenic and the narrative is of a journey, through geography and theology, a journey which penetrates the heart of what it means to be free. Characters have speeches, even soliloquies, which at times seem Shakespearean in their uncovering of thought-process, of personality. Above all, the piece contains not one, but three, maybe even four, tragic heroes, characters who induce empathy, understanding, who are essentially human.

Once I realised that the poem could form the basis for a piece of theatre and began to see how structurally this might be achieved, my task became one of selection. I'm interested in what made Milton want to tell this story in the 1660s and what makes us want to tell it now. Milton explores not only free will, but also the drama of democracy. It is, perhaps, this element of the work which feels most relevant in 2006. Satan's initial insurrection in heaven is a response to what he sees as the unfair installation of Christ at his father's right hand. As with Shakespeare's Iago, who rues that, under Othello, "Preferment goes by letter and affection / And not by old gradation", Satan feels that the essential democracy of heaven has been ignored. It's notable that his own council in hell *is*, on the surface at least, democratic. Different points of view are aired and a consensus is reached. When tempting Eve, Satan again uses the promise of democracy, of knowledge, of an equality of understanding, to lure her into eating the apple. For Milton, writing just seven years after the restoration of the English monarchy, the questions of theocracy versus democracy and the dangers of challenging the divine with humanist political doctrine were relevant and prescient. They feel no less so today.

Recent adaptations of other non-dramatic texts (most notably Andrew Davies' remarkable *Bleak House*), have proved that the key to success in such work is the location of a new dramatic heart which adds to, rather than compromises, the style and tone of the original. It is this which I have sought in my new version of *Paradise Lost*. Whether this endeavour has been successful is for others to say, but everyone involved has embarked with a boldness and an ambition which I fancy Milton would have recognised.

The adaptation process is one that goes on even as I write this, in the middle of rehearsals. It has been joyously collaborative and my endless thanks go to Rupert Goold and his actors, who have frequently shown the wood when all I could see was trees.

Ben Power
March 2006

the RSC; a national and international tour of *Scaramouche Jones* with Pete Postlethwaite; and in August 2006 he will direct *The Tempest* with Patrick Stewart as Prospero for the RSC. His opera work includes *Le Comte Ory* (Garsington Opera) and *L'Opera Seria, Gli Equivoci* and *Il Pomo D'Oro* (Batignano). He will direct *Donna Del Largo* for Garsington Opera in 2007.

Ben Stones Designer

Ben studied at the Electric Theatre Studios, Barnsley, and subsequently trained in stage design at Central Saint Martin's College of Art and Design. In 2003 he was the winner of the Linbury Biennial Prize, commissioned to design *Paradise Lost* for Northampton Theatres. Designs include: *Paradise Lost* (Royal, Northampton); *The Shooky* (Birmingham Rep); *Someone Who'll Watch Over Me* (Royal, Northampton); *Vermilion Dream* (Salisbury Playhouse); *Riders To The Sea* (Southwark Playhouse); *The Marriage Of Bette And Boo* (RADA); *Heads You Lose* (Shaw Theatre); *The Arab Israeli Cookbook* (Tricycle Theatre); *Beautiful Thing* (Sound Theatre); *The Mighty Boosh* (Phil McIntyre national tour). Future Designs include: *Monkey!* (Dundee Rep Theatre) and a revival of *Beautiful Thing* (Sound Theatre).

Mark Jonathan

Lighting Designer

Mark Jonathan has extensive experience as a lighting designer of drama, opera, ballet and musicals in Britain, USA, Europe, The Middle and Far East. He was Head of Lighting at the National Theatre from 1993 until 2003 and has just been appointed Associate

Lighting Designer for the 2006 Chichester Festival. Design credits include *Hamlet* (Northampton); *The Clean House* and *Shadow Mouth* (Crucible Sheffield); *The Wizard of Oz* (Birmingham Rep/West Yorkshire Playhouse); *The Lady's Not for Burning* (Chichester); *Les Liaisons Dangereuses* (Bristol Old Vic); *Cinderella, La Sylphide* and *Sylvia* (Royal Ballet/Royal Opera House); *Beauty and the Beast, Giselle, Sleeping Beauty, Far From the Madding Crowd, The Seasons, Protecting Veil* (Birmingham Royal Ballet); *The Witches* (Birmingham/West End/UK tour); *Ariadne auf Naxos, Falstaff, Peter Grimes* (Los Angeles Opera) as well as many productions at the Royal Court, The Gate, Birmingham Rep, Israeli Opera and American Ballet Theatre. Future productions include *The Sleeping Beauty* (Royal Ballet); *Nicholas Nickleby* (Chichester); *Cyrano* (Birmingham Royal Ballet); *Salomé* (Bavarian State Opera); *Gianni Schicci, Bluebeard's Castle* (Washington Opera).

Liam Steel Choreographer

Liam is joint Artistic Director of Stan Won't Dance and works as a performer, director and choreographer, performing the role of Robert in the original tours of Sinner. For eight years he was a core member of DV8 Physical Theatre as both a performer and Assistant Director of the company. Productions worked on included *MSM; Enter Achilles* (including the award-winning film version); *Bound to Please; The Happiest Day of My Life* and *The Cost of Living*. Other performance credits include work with Nottingham Playhouse, The Royal Court, Manchester Royal Exchange, The Kosh, Volcano Theatre Co, Roundabout Theatre Co, Gay Sweatshop, Theatr Powys, Footloose Dance Company (Powys Dance), Nigel Charnock and Company, Theatre Centre, Frantic Assembly, Royal National Theatre Studio, Graeae Theatre Co, The David Glass Ensemble and Complicite.

Recent directorial/choreographic work includes *Dirty Wonderland* (Brighton International Festival/ Frantic Assembly); *Hymns* (Revised version, 2005 and original, 1999 for Lyric Hammersmith/ Frantic Assembly); *Paradise Lost,* Northampton Theatre Royal; *Pericles,* RSC/Cardboard Citizens Theatre Co; *Strictly Dandia,* Tamasha Theatre Co /Lyric Hammersmith; *The Shooky,* Birmingham Repertory Theatre; *Devotion,* Theatre Centre; *Frankenstein,* Blue Eyed Soul Dance Company; *Heavenly,* Frantic Assembly/Soho Theatre; *Vurt,* Contact Theatre Manchester; The Fall of the House of Usher, Graeae Theatre Company; Look at Me, Theatre Centre; *Sparkleshark,* Royal National Theatre; *The Flight*, Restless Dance Co. (Adelaide Festival-Australia); *15 Degrees and Rising,* Circus Space; *The Secret Garden; Beauty and the Beast; Tom's Midnight Garden, The Ghosts of Scrooge,* Library Theatre, Manchester. He is currently creating *Knots* for Cois Ceim Dance Theatre/Dublin Theatre Festival and will be doing *Oliver Twist* for the Library Theatre.

Georgina Lamb
Choreographer

Georgina Lamb works as a director, choreographer and actor. She is Creative Associate of Frantic Assembly and has worked extensively with the company as a collaborator and performer. Other directing credits include Lyric Hammersmith, Jackson's Lane, Battersea Arts Centre, Pleasance Edinburgh, National Youth Theatre, OnO Theatre Co, West Sussex Youth Theatre, The Baltic, Newcastle and Bigfoot/ London Talent. As movement director / choreographer, credits include Oily Cart, Jet Theatre Co, Half Moon Young People's Theatre, Manchester Met School of Theatre, The Cresset Peterborough and The Work Collective. Performing credits include National Theatre of Scotland, Frantic Assembly, Stephen Joseph Theatre Scarborough, Trestle, Leicester Haymarket, Lyric Hammersmith, Royal Opera House, Library Manchester, Pilot, Fecund Theatre, Gecko and RNT Studio.

Adam Cork
Composer and Sound Designer

Adam Cork studied piano with Jeremy Brown and read music at Cambridge, studying composition with Robin Holloway.
Theatre: Adam has composed music and sound scores for *Caligula, Henry IV* (Donmar Warehouse); *Suddenly Last Summer* (Albery), for which he was nominated for the 2005 Olivier Award for Best Sound Design; *Five Gold Rings* (Almeida); *Scaramouche Jones* (Riverside Studios, Australian and North American tour 2003); *Troilus and Cressida* (Old Vic); *Sunday Father* (Hampstead Theatre); *A Midsummer Night's Dream, Lear* (Sheffield

Crucible); *Alice's Adventures in Wonderland* (Bristol Old Vic); *Romeo and Juliet* (No. 1 tour); *Bedtime Stories* (Stephen Joseph); *My Uncle Arly* (Royal Opera House Linbury Studio); *Insignificance* (Brighton Festival); *The Rise and Fall of Little Voice, Hysteria* (Salisbury Playhouse); *Othello* (Greenwich Theatre); *Broken Glass* (Watford Palace); *Arcadia, The Weir, Waiting for Godot, Paradise Lost, Faustus, Hamlet* (Northampton Royal); *The School for Scandal* (Derby Playhouse); *A Streetcar Named Desire, Blithe Spirit, The Crucible, The Tempest, Blood Wedding, The Dance of Death, The Caucasian Chalk Circle, Romeo and Juliet, The Three Sisters, Macbeth* (Colchester Mercury); *The Colonel-Bird* (Gate); *The End of the Affair* (Bridewell); *Marry Maria* (Hoipolloi); *Arms and the Man* (Northcott Exeter); *2:18 Underground* (Lyric Hammersmith studio); *Alice Through the Looking Glass* (Creation Theatre). **Film/TV:** *Frances Tuesday* (ITV1), *Re-ignited* (Channel 4), *Bust* (Film Council), *Sexdrive* (Vancouver Film Festival), *Tripletake* (JJC Films). **Radio:** *Losing Rosalind* (BBC Radio 4), *The Colonel-Bird* (BBC World Service).

Lorna Heavey
Video Designer

Lorna Heavey is a video artist interested in exploring the integration of disciplines, collaboration, the transformation of space and meaning derived from unexpected combinations within theatre, music, installation and performance.
She studied Fine Art at Düsseldorf Academy, (class of Nan June Paik and Nan Hoover), Kingston, and Chelsea School of Art. She was elected Fellow of the Royal Society of Arts in 2004.
She is currently working on a production of *The Caucasian Chalk Circle* with Filter Theatre for the National Theatre. Recently for theatre she has designed video for *Phaedra* (Donmar), *Speaking Like Magpies* (RSC), *Vanishing Points* (Complicite, German Gym), *Genoa 01* (Complicite, Royal Court), *Paradise Lost, Betrayal* (Theatre Royal, Northampton), *Cleansed* (Arcola), *Cooped* (National Theatre and international tour), *Tall Phoenix* (Belgrade), *Newsnight The Opera, The Waves, The Very Opera* (BAC), *I Am Thicker Than Water* (National Tour). Exhibitions include *Dada Dandies*, Berlin, *Aquaphilia*, R.I.B.A., *Members*, I.C.A., *Trajectory*, UK and European tour. TV and film include *Timed Existence*, (Edinburgh Film Festival), *Several Words* (Split and Hanover Film Festivals), *The Bendix Report* (C4) *The Mighty Boosh* (BBC).

Oxford Stage Company

'Oxford Stage Company has been one of the great success stories of recent years' *The Daily Telegraph*

Oxford Stage Company is dedicated to new ways of making theatre. By exploring the revolutionary writers of the past and commissioning work from the visionary artists of today, we aim to push the imaginative possibilities of the stage. OSC is committed to producing exhilarating, provocative and spectacular theatre to take around the country and around the world.

Artistic Director	Rupert Goold
Executive Producer	Henny Finch
Finance Manager	Helen Hillman
Literary Associate	Ben Power
Administrator / Trainee Producer	Jenni Kershaw
Education Associate	Jacqui Somerville

For more information on future productions or to join our free mailing list, please call 020 7438 9940.

Oxford Stage Company would like to thank all our Friends and especially our Favourites: John and Margaret Lynch, Muriel E.B. Quinn and Uncle Honza.

Oxford Stage Company
Chertsey Chambers, 12 Mercer Street, London, WC2H 9QD
Tel: 020 7438 9940 Fax: 020 7438 9941
E-mail: info@oxfordstage.co.uk
Visit our website at: www.oxfordstage.co.uk

Oxford Stage Company is supported by

Watford Palace Theatre

Watford Palace Theatre re-opened in September 2004 following a major £8.8m Lottery funded refurbishment which saw improvements to the foyer and auditorium areas in addition to increased technical capabilities backstage.

Watford Palace Theatre aims to be a national flagship for artistic, cultural and education provision and focus for creativity for people in Watford, Hertfordshire and beyond. The Theatre's purpose is to create theatre made in Watford of the highest quality and innovation that will excite, delight and inspire…

This is created through the partnership between our audiences and the continued support of our funders – Arts Council England East, Watford Borough Council and Hertfordshire County Council; Children, Schools and Families.

The Palace Theatre has always presented dynamic new plays and since October 2004 has premiered six new or newly adapted plays including a major new musical version of Bill Naughton's novel, *Alfie*. The theatre is committed to supporting new talent, and in 2005 produced writer Ian Kershaw's debut play *Get Ken Barlow*. In association with Paines Plough and the Tron Theatre Glasgow, WPT produced David Greig's latest play *Pyrenees* which went on to win the TMA award for best new play. In 2006, WPT will continue its work with other exciting production companies including Hoipolloi and Oxford Stage Company.

Executive Director	Mary Caws
Literary Director	Joyce Branagh
Associate Director (Active)	Kirstie Davis
Production Manager	Ali Fellows
Development Manager	Jane Foy
Theatre Manager	Kate McCarthy
Head of Sales and Marketing	Craig Titley
Head of Finance	Lucy Williams

Watford Palace Theatre, Clarendon Road, Watford, WD17 1JZ
Administration 01923 235455 / Box Office 01923 225671
www.watfordpalacetheatre.co.uk

PARADISE LOST

First published in this adaptation in 2006 by Oberon Books Ltd
521 Caledonian Road, London N7 9RH
Tel: 020 7607 3637 / Fax: 020 7607 3629
e-mail: info@oberonbooks.com
www.oberonbooks.com

A catalogue record for this book is available from the British
Library.

Cover photograph by Ben Stones; cover design by SWD

ISBN: 1 84002 666 9

Printed in Great Britain by Antony Rowe Ltd, Chippenham.

Characters

THE SON

SATAN

BEELZEBUB

MOLOCH

BELIAL

DEATH

SIN

CHAOS

The voice of GOD

RAPHAEL

ADAM

EVE

GABRIEL

This adaptation was first performed on 30 January 2004 at the Royal Theatre, Northampton, with the following cast:

Christian Bradley
Antony Bunsee
Darrell D'Silva
Caroline Faber
Leah Muller
Jonjo O'Neill

Director Rupert Goold
Designer Ben Stones
Lighting Designer Neil Austin
Music and Sound Designer Adam Cork
Choreographer Liam Steel
Video Designer Lorna Heavey

Prologue

An empty stage. Enter THE SON. His hands are bandaged. In silence, he dances. His movement gets faster and more frantic until, suddenly, it stops.

THE SON

Sing heavenly Muse!
Of Man's first disobedience, and the fruit
Of that forbidden tree, whose mortal taste
Brought death into the world and all our woe,
Sing!
What in us is dark,
Illume; what is low, raise and support;
That to the height of this great argument
We may assert eternal providence,
And justify the ways of God to men.
Say first what cause
Moved our grandparents in that happy state,
Favoured of Heaven so highly, to fall off
From their creator, and transgress His will?
Who first seduced them to that foul revolt?
The infernal serpent; he it was, whose guile
Stirred up with envy and revenge, deceived
The mother of mankind. Once an angel,
By the name of Satan now known,
He stirred rebellion by aspiring
To set himself in glory above his peers.
Thus he opposed, and with ambitious aim,
The throne and monarchy of God,
Raised impious war on high and battled proud
In vain attempt to equal the highest.
For this was cast from Heaven, with all his host

Of rebel angels. Him the Almighty Power
Hurled headlong flaming from the ethereal sky
With hideous ruin and combustion down
To bottomless perdition, there to dwell
In adamantine chains and penal fire.
A dungeon horrible, on all sides round
As one great furnace flamed, yet from those flames
No light, but rather darkness visible.
Where peace can never dwell, hope never come
That comes to all, but torture without end.
Such place eternal justice had prepared
For those rebellious, here their prison ordained.
Nine times the space that measures day and night
To mortal men, he with his horrid crew,
Lay vanquished, rolling in the fiery gulf.

The stage flares into light and we see rebel angels
falling from Heaven.

Act One

HELL

Lights rise on a lake of fire.

SATAN

O, how fallen! How changed
From him who in the happy realms of light,
Clothed with transcendent brightness, didst out-shine
Myriads!
O how unlike the place from whence we fell!
The companions of my fall, overwhelmed,
Joined with me once, now misery hath joined
In equal ruin.

BEELZEBUB (*Rising.*)

O prince, O chief of many throned powers,
Too well I see and rue the dire event,
That with sad overthrow and foul defeat
Hath lost us Heaven and all this mighty host
In horrible destruction laid thus low.
All our glory extinct. Eternal beings
Shall undergo eternal punishment.

SATAN

What if the field be lost?
All is not lost; the unconquerable will,
And study of revenge, immortal hate,
That glory never shall His wrath or might
Extort from me.
The sulphurous hail and thunder shot in storm,
Ceases now to bellow rage.

Seest thou yon dreary plain, forlorn and wild,
The seat of desolation, void of light,
Thither let us tend, from off these fire-waves
And, reassembling our afflicted powers,
Consult how we may henceforth most offend
Our enemy, our own loss how repair.

THE SON

So the angel, called Satan, though in pain,
Vaunting aloud, but racked with deep despair,
Forthwith rose upright from off the pool
And with expanded wings he steered his flight
Aloft, incumbant on the dusky air.
And following him came his nearest mate,
One next himself in power, and next in crime,
Long after known in Palestine and named
Beelzebub.
On dry land they lighted. A land that burned
With solid, as the lake with liquid, fire.
Such resting found the soles of unblest feet.
Yet both gloried to escape the Stygian flood.

SATAN and BEELZEBUB move off the lake.

SATAN

Is this the region, this the soil, the clime,
That we must change for Heaven, this mournful gloom
For that celestial light? Be it so. And cry:
Farewell happy fields where joy forever dwells!
Hail horrors, hail infernal world, and Hell
Receive thy new possessor – one who brings
A mind not to be changed by place or time.
The mind is its own place, and in itself
Can make a Heaven of Hell, a Hell of Heaven.

What matter where, if I be still the same,
And what I should be, all but less than he
Whom thunder hath made greater? Here at least
We shall be free; the Almighty hath not built
Here for His envy, will not drive us hence.
Here we may reign secure; and, in my choice,
To reign is worth ambition, though in Hell:
Better to reign in Hell than serve in Heaven.

BEELZEBUB

Leader of those armies bright, call forth
The associates and co-partners of our loss.
Once they hear thy voice, their surest signal,
They'll soon resume new courage and revive,
Though they lie prostrate on yon lake of fire.

SATAN

Princes, potentates, the flowers of Heaven,
Once yours, now lost. Have ye chosen this place
After the toil of battle to repose?
Or in this abject posture have ye sworn
To adore the conqueror?
Awake, arise, or be for ever fallen!

THE SON

They heard, and were abashed, and up they sprung,
Roused from the slumber, on that fiery couch,
And came at once to where he stood.

The fallen angels begin to move towards SATAN.

Not far, a hill belched fire and rolling smoke.
Thither, winged with speed, a brigade hastened.
Led by Mammon, the least erected spirit,

And with great toil and hands innumerable,
Soon had his crew opened a spacious wound.
This cave, a dank and muddied retreat,
Was called Pandaemonium, the capital
Of Satan and his peers.

SATAN, BEELZEBUB, MOLOCH and BELIAL
face the audience.

SATAN

O myriads of immortal spirits, O powers
Matchless, but with the Almighty. Know, that strife
Was not inglorious, though the event was dire
As this place testifies, and this dire change
Hateful to utter. But what power of mind
Foreseeing or presaging, from the depth
Of knowledge past or present, could have feared,
How such united force of gods, how such
As stood like these, could ever know repulse?
Henceforth His might we know, and know our own.
This damned infernal pit shall never hold
Celestial spirits in bondage, nor the abyss
Long under darkness cover.
O deities of Heaven, though oppressed and fallen,
I take not Heaven as lost. From this descent,
Celestial virtues rising, will appear
More glorious and more dread than from no fall.
But these thoughts full counsel must mature.
Though me just right, and the fixed laws of Heaven
Did first create your leader; next, free choice
Shall decide by what means we now return
To claim our just inheritance of old.
Whether with open war or covert guile,

We now debate. Who can advise, may speak.
Moloch, sceptered king, put forth thy mind.

MOLOCH

My sentence is for open war. Of wiles
More unexpert, I can boast not: let those
Contrive who need, and when they need, not now.
For while they sit contriving, shall the rest,
Millions that stand in arms, longing, wait as
Heaven's fugitives, and for their dwelling place
Accept this dark opprobious den of shame?
No, let us rather choose to proudly go
Armed with hell-flames and fury all at once
Turning our tortures into horrid arms
Against the torturer. Infernal thunder,
Black fire and horror shot with equal rage.
I know the event is feared: should we provoke
Our stronger, some worse way His wrath may find
To our destruction. But what can be worse
Than to dwell here, driven out from bliss, condemned
In this abhorred deep to utter woe;
Where pain of unextinguishable fire
Must exercise us without hope of end?
What fear we, then?
For if our substance be indeed divine,
And cannot cease to be, then by proof we know
Our power sufficient to disturb His Heaven!

SATAN

Moloch, thy looks denounce desperate revenge
And battle dangerous to less than gods.
Speak Belial, for thy tongue drops manna.
Speak.

BELIAL

I should be much for open war, O peers,
As not behind in hate; if what was urged
Main reason to persuade immediate war,
Did not dissuade me most. First, what revenge?
The towers of Heaven are filled with armed watch,
That render all access impregnable.
And if we could enter, all Hell rising
With blackest insurrection, to confound
Heaven's purest light, yet our great enemy
Unpolluted, would on His throne still sit
Victorious. Thus repulsed, our final hope
Is flat despair; we must exasperate
The Almighty Victor to spend all His rage,
And that must end us, that must be our cure.
To be no more; to perish rather, lost
In the wide womb of uncreated night.
Say they who counsel war, we are so low
What can we suffer worse? Is this the worst,
Thus sitting, thus consulting, thus in arms?
What when we fled, struck with Heaven's thunder?
The deep was then a shelter to us, Hell
A refuge from those wounds. Or when we lay
Chained on the burning lake? That sure was worse.
War therefore, open or concealed, alike
My voice dissuades; for what can force or guile
With Him, or who deceive His mind, whose eye
Sees all actions in one view? This is now
Our doom, which if we can sustain and bear,
This horror will grow mild, this darkness light.

BEELZEBUB

Belial advises peaceful ease and
Ignoble sloth. Our ethereal virtues

Must we renounce and, changing style, be called
Princes of Hell?

SATAN

Fallen cherubs, to be weak is miserable.
To bow and sue for grace were low indeed.
Now, through experience of this great event,
In arms not worse, in foresight much advanced,
We may with more successful hope resolve
To wage, by force or guile, eternal war.
Space may produce new worlds; whereof so rife
There went rumour in Heaven that He, ere long,
Meant there to create a generation,
In regard equal to the sons of Heaven.
Our first eruption should aim only there.
Of this be sure:
To do ought good never will be our task,
But ever to do ill our sole delight.

BEELZEBUB

My lord, imperial power, off-spring of Heaven,
Let me speak.
Let us recognise
This place our dungeon, not our safe retreat.
Why sit we here projecting peace or war?
War hath determined and foiled us with loss.
And as for peace?
What peace for us but severe custody?
And stripes and arbitary punishment.
Is this our fate?
Heaven's high walls fear no assault or siege
Or ambush from the deep. What if we find
Some easier enterprize? There is a place
(If ancient and prophetic fame in Heaven

Err not) another world, the happy seat
Of some new race called Man, about this time
To be created like to us, though less
In power and excellence, but favoured more
Of Him who rules above, so it was told.
Thither let us bend all our thoughts, to learn
What creatures there inhabit, of what mould,
Or substance, how endued, and what their power,
And where their weakness, how attempted best,
By force or subtlety: though Heaven be shut,
And Heaven's high arbitrator sit secure
In His own strength, this place may lie exposed.

SATAN

Think, my devilish council, of our delight
In the act here told; to confound the race
Of mankind in one root, and Earth with Hell
To mingle and involve. Either hell-fire
To waste His whole creation, or possess
All as our own, and drive as we were driven,
The puny habitants. Or, if not drive,
Seduce them to our party, that their God
May prove their foe, and with repenting hand
Abolish His own works. This would surpass
Common revenge and interrupt His joy
In our confusion, with our joy upraised
By His disturbance when His darling sons,
Dragged downwards to partake with us, shall curse
Their frail maker. Advise if this be worth
Attempting, or if we'll sit in darkness
Hatching vain empires. Come, show thy minds.

The fallen angels show their assent.

BEELZEBUB

Well have ye judged, well ended long debate,
Synod of gods, and like to what ye are,
Great things resolved, which, from the lowest deep,
Will once more lift us up, in spite of fate
And purge this gloom. But first, whom shall we send
In search of this new world, whom shall we find
Sufficient? Who shall tempt with wandering feet
The dark unbottomed infinite abyss?

SATAN

Wisely let us choose, for on whom we send,
The weight of all and our last hope relies.

Pause.

BEELZEBUB

Can it be none among the choice and prime
Of these Heaven-warring champions will prove
So hardy as to proffer or accept?
Again, who is it we shall find sufficient?

Pause.

SATAN

So. None will accept alone the dreadful task.
O progeny of Heaven. Long is the way
And hard, that out of Hell leads up to light,
Our prison's strong, a huge convex of fire.
But I should ill become this throne, O peers,
And this imperial sovereignty, adorned
With splendour, armed with power, if aught proposed
And judged of public moment, out of fear

Of difficulty or danger, I did fail
To attempt and lead in the attempting.
For I am lord here and I do assume
These royalties, and not refuse to reign,
Accepting as great a share of hazard
As of honour. Go, therefore, mighty powers,
Terrors of Heaven, though fallen, intend at home,
What best may ease the present misery
And render this place more tolerable.
While I abroad
Through all the coasts of dark destruction seek
Deliverance for us all. This enterprise
None shall partake but me.

    A moment, then:

None shall partake but me.

THE SON

Thus saying rose
The monarch and prevented all reply.
He rised, heading for the void profound,
And left that place of hellish rule behind.
O wretched Man! He comes that wouldst seduce,
Leading thee unto his own damnation.

    SATAN disappears.

Act Two

Dim light on THE SON.

THE SON

Look on, O Muse, and you who bare witness,
With shuddering horror pale, and eyes agast.
View first this lamentable place called Hell.
Rocks, caves, lakes, fens, bogs, dens, and shades of death.
A universe of death, which God by curse
Created evil, for evil only good,
Where all life dies, death lives, and nature breeds.

Lights rise on an large set of gates and two figures.

Here, bars high-reaching to the horrid roof,
Lay the threefold gates of hell. Three were brass,
Three iron, three of adamantine rock.
Impenetrable, impaled with circling fire,
Yet unconsumed. Before the gates there sat
On either side a formidable shape.

Enter SATAN behind.

Meanwhile the adversary of God and Man,
Satan, with thoughts inflamed of highest design,
Put on swift wings, and toward the gates of hell
Explored his solitary flight. Sometimes
He scoured the right-hand coast, sometimes the left,
First shaved with level wing the deep, then soared
Up to the fiery concave towering high.

One of the figures bars SATAN's way.

SATAN

Whence and what art thou, execrable shape
That darest, though grim, to cross my way
To yonder gates?

DEATH

Art thou the traitor angel? Art thou he
Who first broke peace with arms 'gainst Heaven and faith,
For which thou, cast from God, are here condemned
To waste eternal days in woe and pain?

SATAN

Through yonder bounds I mean to pass unchecked.
Retire or taste thy folly, and learn by proof,
Hell-born, not to contend with spirits of Heaven.

DEATH

Dost reckonest thou thyself a spirit of Heaven
When I reign king and what is more, thy lord?
Back to thy punishment false fugitive,
Lest with a whip of scorpians I pursue
Thy lingering, or with one stroke of this dart
Strange horrors seize thee with pangs unfelt before.

SATAN

Retire or taste thy folly, terrible shape.

*SATAN is ready to charge, when the other figure
intervenes.*

SIN

O father! What intends thy hand, thy wrath,
Against thy only son? What fury, O son,
Possesses thee to bend that mortal dart
Against thy father's head? And knowest for whom?
For Him that sits above and readies now
His wrath which one day will destroy ye both!

SATAN

So strange thy outcry and thy words so strange
Thou interposest, my sudden hand halts
What it intends, 'til first I know of thee:
What thing thou art and why, first met, thou callst
Me father and that phantasm callst my son?

SIN

Hast thou forgot me, then?

SATAN

I know thee not, nor ever saw 'til now
Sight more detestable than him and thee.

SIN

Now in thine eye so foul, once deemed so fair
In Heaven. Canst thou not recall the time when
All on a sudden, miserable pain
Surprised thee, dimmed thine eyes, which, dizzy, swum
In darkness? Thy head flaming thick and fast,
On the left side opening wide, threw forth one
Likest to thee in shape and countenance bright.
Out of thy head I sprung, a goddess armed.
Afraid, thou recoiled first and called me Sin,
Portentous held me. But, familiar grown,

I pleased, and with my graces full soon thou
Becamest enamoured, and such joy thou tookst
With me in secret, that my womb conceived
A growing burden. Meanwhile war arose,
And fields were fought in Heaven, wherein remained,
For what else could, to our almighty foe
Clear victory, to our part loss and rout.
Driven headlong from the pitch of Heaven, down
Into this deep thy whole assembly fell.
Down I came also; at which time this key
Into my hand was given, with charge to keep
These gates forever shut, which none can pass
Without my opening. Pensive here I sat
Alone, but long I sat not, 'til my womb
Pregnant by thee, prodigious motion felt.
At last this odious offspring whom thou seest,
Thine own begotten, breaking violent way,
Tore through my entrails, that with fear and pain
Distorted, all my nether shape thus grew
Transformed.
I fled, afraid of him, and cried out 'Death'.
Hell trembled at the hideous name, and sighed
From all her caves, and back resounded 'Death'.
I fled, but he pursued, and, swifter far,
Soon overtook his mother all dismaid
And in embraces forcible and foul
Ingendered with me. Of that rape begot
These yelling monsters, that with ceaseless cry
Surround us, causing sorrow infinite
To me. For when they list into the womb
That bred them they return, and howl and gnaw
My bowels. This done then they come bursting forth
Afresh with terrors and so vex me round,
That rest or intermission find I none.

But thou O father, I forewarn thee, shun
That deadly arrow. Do not vainly hope
To be invulnerable in those bright arms,
Though tempered heavenly, for that mortal blow,
Save He who reigns above, none can resist.

SATAN

Dear daughter, since thou claimst me for thy sire,
And my fair son here showst me, the dear pledge
Of dalliance I had with thee in Heaven, know
I come no enemy, but to set free
From out this dark and dismal house of pain,
Both him and thee, and all the heavenly host
Which fell with me from high.

SIN

The key of this infernal pit, by due,
And by command of Heaven's all-powerful King
I keep, by Him forbidden to unlock
These adamantine gates.

SATAN

From here I go
To search with wandering quest a place of bliss.
Wherein exists, if rumour be proved true,
A race of upstart creatures, made to take,
Perhaps, our vacant place. If this be true
I shall make nuisance and tempt them from Him,
Their creator. Once done, I'll soon return
And bring ye to the place where thou and Death
Shall dwell at ease, and up and down unseen
Wing silently the buxom air.
There ye shall be fed and filled immeasurably,
All things shall be your prey.

SIN

What owe I then to His commands above
Who hates me, and hath hither thrust me down
To sit in hateful office here confined?
Thou art my father, thou my author, thou
My being gavest me; whom should I obey
But thee, whom follow? Thou wilt bring me soon
To that new world of light and bliss, among
The gods who live at ease, where I shall reign
At thy right hand, voluptuous, as beseems
Thy daughter and thy darling, without end.

She unlocks the gates. They swing open and SATAN
moves off into the void.

THE SON

Thus saying Sin in that great keyhole turned
The intricate wards, and every bolt and bar
Of massy iron or solid rock with ease
Then unfastened. In one swift moment flew
With impetuous recoil and jarring sound
The infernal doors, and their hinges grated
Harsh thunder.
So wide they stood and like a furnace mouth
Cast forth redounding smoke and ruddy flame.
And now, O Muse, bring forth to sudden view
The secrets of the hoary deep, a dark
Illimitable ocean without bound,
Without dimension, where length, breadth and height,
And time and place are lost. Where eldest Night
And Chaos, ancestors of nature, hold
Eternal anarchy, amidst the noise
Of endless war and ever-shrieking wrath.

The stage rings with strange noises.

Into this wild abyss,
The womb of nature and, perhaps, her grave,
Of neither water, earth, air nor fire made,
But all these in their pregnant causes mixed
Confusedly, which thus must always fight
Unless the Almighty Maker them ordain
His dark materials to create more worlds.

SATAN

Into this wild abyss, the weary fiend
Stood on the brink of Hell and looked awhile
Pondering his voyage, for no narrow frith
Had he to cross. At last his sail-broad wings
He spread for flight and, in the surging smoke,
Uplifted spurned the ground. He rose at first, then,
Meeting a vast vacuum, straight down he dropped
Ten thousand fathoms deep.

THE SON

The strong rebuff of some tumultuous cloud
Instinct with fire and nitre hurried him
As many miles aloft, 'til Satan stayed
Quenched in a boggy syrtis, neither sea
Nor good dry land.

SATAN moves through the void.

SATAN

Now through the crude consistence moved the fiend.
Over bog or steep, through straight, rough, dense or rare
With head, hands, wings or feet pursued his way,
And swam or sank or waded, or crept or flew.

THE SON

At length a universal hubbub wild
Of stunning sounds and voices all confused
Born through the hollow dark assaulted his ear
With loudest vehemence.

SATAN

Thither he plied
Undaunted to meet whatever power
Might in that noise reside and ask of it
Which way the nearest coast of darkness lay,
Bordering on light.

Enter CHAOS.

THE SON

He beheld the faces
Of Chaos, their sable-vested shapes spread
Wide on the wasteful deep,
Crying fierce discord with a thousand mouths.

SATAN

Ye powers!
Ye spirits of Chaos and ancient Night,
I come no spy with purpose to disturb
The secrets of your realm, but by constraint
I wander this dark desert. For my way
Lies through your spacious empire up to light.
Alone and without guide, half-lost, I seek
What readiest path leads where your gloomy bounds
Join up to Heaven and there another place
Created lately by the Ethereal King.
There I aim to arrive. Direct my course!

CHAOS

Chaos knows thee stranger and who thou art.
That mighty leading angel, who, of late,
Made war 'gainst Heaven's King, though overthrown.
We saw and heard, for such a numerous host
Fled not in silence through the frighted deep.
We here reside, upon our far frontiers,
Where lately there appeared another world, Earth,
Hanging over our realm and linked with gold chains
To that side Heaven from whence your regions fell.
If that way be your walk you have not far.
Go and speed.

Exit CHAOS.

SATAN

Satan stayed not to question those voices
But, glad that now his sea might find a shore,
Sprung upwards like a pyramid of fire
Into the wild expanse, and, through the shock
Of fighting elements, on all sides round
Environed, won his way.

THE SON

A dark and lonely void, with boiling gulf,
The fiend now passed as he moved through limbo.
And long he wandered, 'til at last a gleam
Of light appeared with a glimmering dawn.
He turned his travelled steps toward that beam
And ere long in the distance there appeared,
Ascending by degrees magnificent
Up to the wall of Heaven, a structure high,
At top whereof, but far more rich, appeared
The work of a kingly palace gate.

Lights reveal a golden ladder.

The stairs were such as whereon Jacob saw
Bright angels ascending and descending
As he dreamt by night under open skies
And, waking, cried, 'This is the gate of Heaven'.
The steps were there let down, whether to dare
The fiend by easy ascent, or aggravate
His sad exclusion from the doors of bliss.

SATAN

And Satan, pausing only to reflect
On that stair's splendour and the wealth of Heaven
To him forever denied, rose up until
He stood there on the lowest shining perch
That scaled by steps of gold to Heaven gate.
And, turning from the gates, looked down with awe.

*SATAN climbs the ladder and looks down at the
universe beneath him.*

THE SON

There all the universe extended wide,
In circuit undetermined square or round.
He looked at the sudden view and saw that orb
Hanging there which he had sought so long.
This pendant world in bigness as a star
Of smallest magnitude, close by the Moon.

SATAN

As when a scout
Through dark and desert ways with peril gone
All night; at last by break of cheerful dawn

Obtains the brow of some high-climbing hill,
Now such a wonder seized the malign spirit
At sight of all this world beheld so fair.

THE SON

Round he surveyed, and well might, where he stood
So high above the circling canopy
Of night's extended shade; from eastern point
Of Libra, to the fleecey star that bears
Andromeda far off Atlantic seas.
Amongst innumerable stars there shone
Distant other worlds, and above them all
The golden sun, in splendour likest Heaven.

*SATAN jumps down, off into the darkness. The SON
climbs the ladder.*

Now, Almighty Father, from above,
From the pure empyrean where Thou sit'st
High throned above all height, bend down Thine eye,
And now survey
Hell and the gulf between, and Satan here
Coasting the wall of Heaven and ready now
To stoop with wearied wings, and willing feet
On the bare outside of the Earth.

A voice replies:

GOD

Only begotten Son, seest thou what rage
Transports our adversary, whom no bounds
Prescribed, no bars of Hell, can hold.
For now,

Through all restraint broke loose, he wings his way
Not far off Heaven, in the precincts of light,
Directly towards the new created world,
And Man there placed, with purpose to assay
If him by force he can destroy, or worse,
By guile, pervert. And know he shall pervert.
For Man will hearken to his glozing lies,
And easily transgress the sole command,
Sole pledge of his obedience. So will fall
He and his faithless progeny.

THE SON

O Father,
Should Man finally be lost? Should Man
Thy creature late so loved, thy youngest son
Fall?

GOD

Thou speakst as my thoughts are, all
As my eternal purpose hath decreed.

THE SON

That be from Thee far!
That far be from Thee, Father, who art judge
Of all things made, and judgest only right.
Shall the adversary thus obtain
His end, and frustrate Thine? Shall he fulfill
His malice, and Thy goodness bring to naught?
And return with revenge accomplished
And to Hell
Draw after him the whole race of mankind,
By him corrupted?

GOD

Whose fault?
Whose but his own? Ingrate, he had of me
All he could have. I made him just and right,
Sufficient to stand, though free to fall.
Such I created all the ethereal powers.
Freely they stood who stood, and fell who fell.

THE SON

Wilt Thou Thyself
Abolish Thy creation, and unmake,
For those who fell, what Thou hast made?
So should Thy goodness and Thy greatness both
Be questioned and blasphemed without defence.

GOD

They themselves decree their own revolt
Not I, for so
I formed men free, and free they must remain,
'Til they enthral themselves. I else must change
Their nature, and revoke the high decree
Unchangeable, eternal, which ordained
Their freedom.
So losing all,
He with his whole posterity must die.
Unless for him
Some other able, and as willing, pay
This rigid satisfaction: death for death.
Say, Heavenly powers, where shall we find such love?
Which of ye will be mortal to redeem
Man's mortal crime?
Dwells in all Heaven charity so dear?

Silence.

THE SON

He asked but all the Heavenly Choir stood mute
And silence was in Heaven. On man's behalf
Patron or intercessor none appeared.
And now without redemption all mankind
Seems to be lost, adjudged to Death and Hell
By doom severe.

*Lights fade on the ladder and SATAN is revealed
moving below.*

SATAN

Meanwhile Satan, his course he bent.
Through the calm firmament, but up or down
By centre, or eccentric, hard to tell.
He strode the vulgar constellations thick,
That from his lordly eye kept distance due,
Forever their starry dance computing
Days, months and years.

Lights rise on the sun, with RAPHAEL upon it.

THE SON

On that all-clearing lamp
The sun, now landed the fiend.
The place he found beyond expression bright,
Compared with aught on Earth, metal or stone;
Not all parts alike, but all alike informed
With radiant light, as glowing iron with fire,
There in the dark so many precious things
Of colour glorious and effect so rare.
Here matter new to gaze the devil met
Undazed, far and wide his eye commanded

For sight no obstacle found here, nor shade,
But all was sun-shine beams. Whereby he soon
Saw within ken a glorious angel stand.
Glad was the spirit impure as now in hope
To find who might direct his wandering flight
To paradise, the happy seat of man,
His journey's end and our beginning woe.

SATAN

But first he casts to change his proper shape.

He transforms himself into an angelic cherub.

And now a stripling cherub he appears,
Not of the prime, yet such as in his face
Youth smiled celestial and to every limb
Suitable grace diffused.

SATAN climbs to where RAPHAEL stands.

Raphael!
An unspoken desire to see, and know,
All these God's wondrous works, but chiefly Man,
To visit oft His new creation round,
Hath brought me from the Choirs of Cherubim
Alone thus wandering. Brightest Seraph tell
In which of all these shining orbs hath man
His fixed seat,
That I may find him and with secret gaze,
Or open admiration, him behold.
Then both in him and all things, as is meet,
The Universal Maker I may praise
Who justly hath driven out His rebel foes
To deepest Hell and, to repair that loss,

Created this new happy race of men
To serve Him better: wise are all His ways.

THE SON

Now, neither man nor angel can discern
Hypocrisy, the only evil that walks
Invisible, except to God alone.
That evil now beguiled Raphael,
The sharpest sighted spirit of all in Heaven,
Who of the fraudulent impostor thought
No evil there where simple goodness seemed.

RAPHAEL

Fair angel, thy desire which tends to know
The works of God, thereby to glorify
The great Work-Master, leads to no excess
That reaches blame, but rather merits praise.
I saw when, at His word, the formless mass,
This world's material mould, came to a heap.
Confusion heard His voice, and wild uproar
Stood ruled, stood vast infinitude confined,
'Til at His second bidding darkness fled,
Light shone, and order from disorder sprung.
Swift to their several quarters hastened then
The cumbrous elements, earth, flood, air, fire,
And this ethereal quintessence of Heaven
Flew upward, spirited with various forms,
That rolled orbicular, and turned to stars,
Numberless, as thou seest.
Each had his place appointed, each his course,
The rest in circuit wall this universe.
Look downward on that globe whose hither side
With light from hence, though but reflected, shines;
That place is Earth, the seat of man, that light

His day.
The spot to which I point is Paradise,
Adam's abode, those lofty shades, his bower.
Thy way thou canst not miss.

*SATAN moves off towards Mount Niphates and
resumes his normal appearance.*

THE SON

Satan, the tempter, now inflamed with rage,
Came down, and landed on Niphates top,
To wreck on innocent frail Man his loss.
But on that mountain peak he rejoiced not,
For within that breast conscience woke despair
That slumbered, woke the bitter memory
Of what he had been, and what he must be,
Worse; of worse deeds worse sufferings must ensue.

SATAN

O sun, that with surpassing glory crowned,
Lookst from thy sole dominion like the God
Of this new world; at whose sight all the stars
Hide their diminished heads; to thee I call,
But with no friendly voice, and add thy name
O sun, to tell thee how I hate thy beams
That bring to my remembrance from what state
I fell, how glorious once above thy sphere;
'Til pride and, worse, ambition, threw me down.
Warring in Heaven against Heaven's matchless King!
Ah wherefore! He deserved no such return
From me whom He created what I was
In that bright eminence.
Yet all His good proved ill in me,
And wrought but malice. Lifted up so high

I scorned subjection, and thought one step higher
Would set me highest, and in a moment quit
The debt immense of endless gratitude,
Forgetful what from him I still received.
O had His powerful Destiny ordained
Me some inferior angel, I had stood
Then happy, no unbounded hope had raised
Ambition. Yet why not? Some other power
As great might have aspired, and me though mean
Drawn to his part. But other powers as great
Fell not, but stand unshaken, from within
Or from without, to all temptations armed.
Hadst thou the same free will and power to stand?
Thou hadst: whom have I then or what to accuse,
But Heaven's free love dealt equally to all?
Be then His love accursed, since love or hate,
To me alike, it deals eternal woe.
Nay, cursed be me! Since against His my will
Chose freely what it now so justly rues.
Me miserable! Which way shall I fly
Infinite wrath, or infinite despair?
Which way I fly is Hell; myself am Hell;
And in the lowest deep, a lower deep,
Still threatening to devour me, opens wide,
To which the Hell I suffer seems a Heaven.
O then, at last, relent. Is there no place
Left for repentance, none for pardon left?
None left but by submission, and that word
Disdain forbids me, and my dread of shame
Among the spirits beneath, whom I seduced
With other promises and other vaunts
Then to submit, boasting I could subdue
The Omnipotent. Ay me, they little know
How dearly I abide that boast so vain,

Under what torments inwardly I groan,
While they adore me on the throne of Hell.
The lower still I fall, only supreme
In misery. Such joy ambition finds.
But say I could repent and could obtain
By act of grace my former state, how soon
Would height recall high thoughts, how soon unsay
What feigned submission swore? Ease would recant
Vows made in pain, as violent and void
For never can true reconcilement grow
Where wounds of deadly hate have pierced so deep.
This would but lead me to a worse relapse
And heavier fall.
This knows my punisher, therefore as far
From granting He, as I from begging peace.
All hope excluded thus, behold instead
Of us out-cast, exiled, his new delight,
Mankind created, and for him this world.
So farewell hope, and with hope farewell fear.
Farewell remorse. All good to me is lost.
Evil be thou my good, by thee at least
Divided empire with Heaven's King I hold
And over more than half, perhaps, will reign,
As Man ere long, and this new world shall know.

SATAN opens a door at the back of the stage. Beyond is a brilliant green light; Eden. He steps through the door and closes it behind him.

THE SON

Of worse deeds, worse sufferings must ensue.

Slow blackout.

Act Three

Lights rise on Eden, dusk. Enter ADAM and EVE, naked.

ADAM

Thou that madst the night,
Maker omnipotent, and Thou the day,
Which we in our appointed work employed
Hath finished happy in our mutual help
And mutual love, the crown of all our bliss
Ordained by Thee, in this delicious place.

EVE

For us it is too large, yet Thou we trust,
For Thou hast promised from us two a race
To fill the Earth, who shall, with us, extol
Thy goodness infinite, both as we wake,
And when we seek, as now, Thy gift of sleep.

They lie down to sleep.

ADAM

Sole partner and sole part of all these joys,
Oh, let us ever praise Him, the power
That raised us from the dust and set us here.

EVE

My guide, what thou hast said is just and right.
For we to Him indeed all praises owe
And daily thanks.

ADAM

Blessed is He who requires
From us no other service than to keep
This one, this easy, charge: of all the trees
In Paradise that bear delicious fruit
So various, not to taste that only tree
Of Knowledge, planted by the Tree of Life.

EVE

My author and disposer, this I know.
So near grows death to life, whate'er death is,
Some dreadful thing no doubt.

ADAM

God hath pronounced it death to taste that tree.

EVE

The only sign of our obedience left
Among so many signs of power and rule
Conferred on us and dominion given.

ADAM

So let us not think hard
One easy prohibition, who enjoy
Free leave so large to all things else, and choice
Unlimited of manifold tasks.

EVE

What thou and He bidst I freely obey.
Thou, from whom I was formed; flesh of thy flesh;
And without whom am to no purpose bound.
That day I oft remember, when from sleep

I first awaked and found myself reposed
Under a shade of flowers, much wondering where
And what I was, whence thither brought and how.
Not distant far from thence a murmuring sound
Of waters issued from a cave and spread
Into a liquid plain. I thither went
With unexperienced thought and laid me down
On the green bank to look into the clear
Smooth lake, that to me seemed another sky.
As I bent down to look, just opposite,
A shape within the watery gleam appeared,
Bending to look on me. I started back,
It started back, but pleased I soon returned,
Pleased it returned as soon with answering looks
Of sympathy and love. There I had fixed
Mine eyes 'til now, and pined with vain desire,
Had not a voice thus warned me: 'What thou seest,
What there thou seest, fair creature, is thy self.
With thee it came and goes, but follow me,
And I will bring thee where no shadow stays
Thy coming, and thy soft embraces, he
Whose image thou art, him thou shalt enjoy,
Inseparably thine, to him shalt bear
Multitudes like thy self, and thence be called
Mother of human race.' What could I do,
But follow straight, invisibly thus led?
'Til I espied thee, fair indeed and tall,
Under a platan, yet methought less fair,
Less winning soft, less amiably mild,
Than that smooth watery image. Back I turned,
Thou following criedst aloud, 'Return fair Eve,
Whom fliest thou? Whom thou fliest, of him thou art,
His flesh, his bone. To give thee being I lent
Out of my side to thee, nearest my heart,

Substantial life, to have thee by my side,
Henceforth an individual solace dear.
Part of my soul I seek thee, and thee claim
My other half.' With that thy gentle hand
Seized mine, I yielded, and from that time see
How beauty is excelled by manly grace
And wisdom, which alone is truly fair.

ADAM

Fair consort, the hour
Of night, and all things now retired to rest
Mind us of like repose, since God hath set
Labour and rest, as day and night to men
Successive, and the timely dew of sleep
Now falling with soft, slumbrous weight inclines
Our eyelids.
Tomorrow, ere fresh morning streak the East
With first approach of light, we must be risen
And at our pleasant labour, to reform
The flowery arbors, verdant alleys green.
Meanwhile, as nature wills, night bids us rest.

*They sleep as night draws in. GABRIEL is revealed,
above.*

GABRIEL

Besides the Eastern gate of Paradise,
Betwixt two rocky pillars, Gabriel sat,
Chief of the angelic guards, awaiting night.

Enter RAPHAEL.

RAPHAEL

To him came Raphael, gliding through the Heavens,
Swift as a shooting star.

GABRIEL

What bringst thou to me
In such haste from thy sun's bright circle?

RAPHAEL

This day, at height of noon came to my sphere
A spirit, zealous, as he seemed, to know
More of the Almighty's works, and chiefly Man,
God's latest image. I described his course
Bent all on speed, and marked his airy gait.
But on the mount that lies from Eden north
Where he first lighted, soon discerned his looks
Alien from Heaven, with passions foul obscured.
Mine eye pursued him still, but under shade
Lost sight of him. One of the banished crew
I fear, hath ventured from the deep, to raise
New troubles. Him our care must be to find.

GABRIEL

Raphael, no wonder that thy perfect sight,
Amid the sun's bright circle where thou sit'st,
Sees far and wide. In at this gate none pass
The vigilance here placed, but such as come
Well known from Heaven and since meridian hour
No creature thence. If spirit of other sort,
So minded, have overleapt these earthy bounds
On purpose, hard thou knowst it to exclude
Spiritual substance with corporeal bar.
Search through this garden, leave unsearched no nook,

But chiefly where those two fair creatures lodge,
Now laid perhaps asleep secure of harm.
The infernal spirit of whom thou tellst,
If such you find, seize fast and hither bring.

Exit RAPHAEL and GABRIEL, separately. Below,
SATAN enters. Behind him, the SON.

SATAN

O Hell! What do mine eyes with grief behold,
Into this room of bliss thus high advanced?
Creatures of other mould, Earth-born perhaps.
Not spirits, yet to heavenly spirits bright
Little inferior.
Ah gentle pair, ye little think how nigh
Your change approaches, when all these delights
Will vanish and deliver ye to woe,
More woe, the more your taste is now of joy.
Hell shall unfold,
To entertain you two, her widest gates,
And send forth all her kings. There will be room,
Not like these narrow limits, to receive
Your numerous offspring.
Sight hateful, sight tormenting! That these two,
Imparadised in one another's arms,
The happier Eden, should enjoy their fill
Of bliss on bliss, while I to Hell am thrust!
Yet let me not forget what I have gained,
As I listened here, crouched among the trees,
From their own mouths. All is not theirs it seems.
One fatal tree there stands of Knowledge called,
Forbidden them to taste. Knowledge forbidden?
Suspicious, reasonless. Why should their lord
Envy them that? Can it be sin to know?

Can it be death? And do they only stand
By ignorance, is that their happy state,
The proof of their obedience and their faith?
O, fair foundation laid whereon to build
Their ruin! Hence I will excite their minds
With more desire to know, and to reject
Envious commands, invented with design
To keep them low whom knowledge might exalt,
Equal with gods. Aspiring to be such,
They taste and die. What likelier can ensue?

*SATAN moves to the sleeping figures and begins to
whisper in EVE's ear.*

Enter RAPHAEL.

RAPHAEL

Which of those rebel spirits adjudged to Hell
Comest thou, escaped thy prison, and transformed?
Why sit'st thou like an enemy in wait
Here, watching at the head of these that sleep?

SATAN

Know ye not then?
Know ye not me? Ye knew me once for sure.
Not to know me argues yourself unknown.

RAPHAEL

Think not, revolted spirit, thy shape the same,
Or undiminished brightness, to be known
As when thou stoodst in Heaven upright and pure.
That glory then, when thou no more was good,
Departed from thee, and thou resemblest now
Thy sin and place of doom obscure and foul.

But come, for thou, be sure, shalt give account
To Him who sent us, whose charge is to keep
This place inviolable, and these from harm.

SATAN

If I must contend, then let that be so.
Best with the best, the sender not the sent.

They move across to where GABRIEL waits.

RAPHAEL

Gabriel, this fallen creature I found,
Squat like a toad, close at the ear of Eve.

GABRIEL

Why hast thou, Satan, broke the bounds prescribed
To thy transgressions, to violate sleep, and those
Whose dwelling God hath planted here in bliss?

SATAN

Gabriel, thou hadst in Heaven the esteem of wise,
But this question asked puts me in some doubt.
Lives there who loves his pain?
Who would not, finding way, break loose from hell,
Though thither doomed?
Let Him surer bar His great iron gates,
If He intends our stay in that dark durance.

GABRIEL

So wise thou judge it to fly from pain
And escape thy punishment!
But wherefore thou alone? Wherefore with thee
Came not all hell broke loose?

SATAN

Not that I less endure, or shrink from pain,
Insulting angel.

GABRIEL

Is pain to them
Less pain? Less to be fled? Or thou than they
Less hardy to endure? Courageous chief,
The first in flight from pain!

SATAN

What behoves
A faithful leader, not to hazard all
Through ways of danger by himself untried?
I therefore, I alone, first undertook
To wing the desolate abyss, and spy
This new created world in hope to find
Better abode, and my afflicted powers
To settle here on Earth.

GABRIEL

Satan, darest thou 'faithful' add? O name,
O sacred name of faithfulness profaned!
Faithful to whom? To thy rebellious crew?
Army of fiends, fit body to fit head.

SATAN

For possession here we try once more to gain
What thou and thy legions would never dare.

GABRIEL

O thou sly hypocrite, who now wouldst seem
Patron of liberty.

SATAN

Thy easier business is to serve thy lord
High up in Heaven with songs to hymn His throne
And practised distances to cringe, not fight.

GABRIEL

Who more than thou
Once fawned, and cringed, and servilely adored
Heaven's aweful monarch?
Wherefore then didst thou fight, except in hope
To dispossess him, and thyself to reign?
Fly thither whence thou fledst! If, from this hour,
Within these hallowed limits thou appearst,
Back to the infernal pit I'll drag thee chained
And seal thee there, as henceforth not to scorn
The iron gates of Hell as too slightly barred.

SATAN

Then when I am thy captive talk of chains,
Proud limitary cherub, but ere then
Far heavier load thyself expect to feel
From my prevailing arm.

GABRIEL

Satan, I know thy strength, and thou knowest mine,
Neither our own but given. What folly then
To boast what arms can do, since thine no more
Than Heaven permits, nor mine, though doubled now
To trample thee as mire. For proof look up,
And read thy lot in this celestial sign
Where thou art weighed, and shown how light, how weak,
If thou resist.

Bright lights on SATAN who exits. GABRIEL and
RAPHAEL follow. The SON steps forward as the
light of morning rises.

THE SON

Now morn, advancing, rose from Eastern skies,
With brightest steps, drew on that dreadful day.
The day foretold of man's disloyal breech
That brought into this world a world of woe.
Though now from here the shades of night fly far
Soon Sin and Death's approach will call them back.
Now the only sound, leaves and fuming rills
Lightly dispersed and the shrill mating song
Of birds on every bow.

THE SON watches as ADAM awakes.

ADAM

Awake,
My fair espoused, my ever-new delight.
Awake, the morning shines and the fresh field
Calls us. We lose the prime, to mark how spring
Our tended plants, how blows the citron grove
How nature paints her colours.

EVE wakes

EVE

O sole in whom my thoughts find all repose,
My glory, my perfection, glad I see
Thy face, and morn returned, for I this night,
Have dreamed, not as I oft am wont, of thee,
But of offence and trouble. Methought
Close at mine ear one called me forth to walk

With gentle voice, I thought it thine. It said,
'Why sleepst thou Eve? Now is the pleasant time,
The cool, the silent, save where silence yields
To the night-warbling bird. Heaven wakes his eyes,
Whom to behold but thee, nature's desire,
In whose sight all things joy, with ravishment
Attracted by thy beauty still to gaze.'
I rose as at thy call, but saw thee not.
To find thee I directed then my walk,
And on, methought, alone, I passed through ways
That brought me on a sudden to the Tree
Of interdicted Knowledge. Fair it seemed,
Much fairer to my fancy than by day,
And, as I wondering looked, beside it stood
One shaped and winged like one of those from Heaven.
And, 'O fair plant,' said he, 'with fruit surcharged,
Deigns none to ease thy load and taste thy sweet?
Not God, nor man; is knowledge so despised?
Or envy, or what reserve forbids to taste?
Forbid who will, none shall from me withhold
Longer thy offered good, why else set here?'
This said he paused not, but with 'ventrous arm
He plucked, he tasted. Me damp horror chilled
At such bold words vouched with a deed so bold,
But he thus overjoyed, 'O fruit divine,
Sweet of thy self, but much more sweet thus cropped,
Forbidden here, it seems, as only fit
For gods, yet able to make gods of men.
Here, happy creature, fair angelic Eve,
Partake thou also. Happy though thou art,
Happier thou mayst be, worthier canst not be.
Taste this, and be henceforth among the gods.'
So saying, he drew nigh, and to me held,
Even to my mouth, of that same fruit, held part

Which he had plucked. The pleasant savoury smell
So quickened appetite, that I, methought,
Could not but taste. Forthwith up to the clouds
With him I flew, and underneath beheld
The Earth outstretched immense, a prospect wide
And various. Wondering at my flight and change
To this high exaltation, suddenly
My guide was gone, and I, methought, sunk down,
And fell asleep. But O, how glad I waked
To find this but a dream.

ADAM

Best image of myself and dearer half,
The trouble of thy thoughts this night in sleep
Affects me equally. Nor can I like
This uncouth dream, of evil sprung I fear.
Yet evil whence? In thee can harbour none,
Created pure.
'Tis oft, in reason's absence, fancy wakes
To imitate her with misjoining shapes.
Wild works she produces and most in dreams.
Some such resemblances methinks I find
Of our last evening's talk, in this thy dream,
But with addition strange. Yet be not sad.
Evil into the mind of god or man
May come and go, so unapproved, and leave
No spot or blame behind. This gives me hope
That what in sleep thou didst abhor to dream,
Waking thou never wilt consent to do.
Be not disheartened then, nor cloud those looks,
But let us to our fresh employments rise
Among the groves, the fountains, and the flowers.

Enter RAPHAEL.

Native of Heaven, vouchsafe with us
To rest, and what the garden choicest bears
To sit and taste, 'til this meridian heat
Be over, and the sun more cool decline.

RAPHAEL

Adam, I therefore came, nor art thou such
Created, or such place hast here to dwell,
As may not oft invite such spirits of Heaven
To visit thee. Lead on then where thy bower
O'ershades, for these mid-hours, 'til noontime comes,
I have at will.

They sit and ADAM offers food.

ADAM

Heavenly stranger, please to taste
These bounties which our Nourisher descends
To us for food. Unsavoury food perhaps
To spiritual natures.

RAPHAEL

Know, Adam, that food alike our pure
Intelligential substances require
As doth your rational and both contain
Within them every lower faculty
Of sense, whereby they hear, see, smell, touch, taste.
For know, whatever was created needs
To be sustained and fed.

ADAM

Inhabitant with God, say what compare
This earthly place with that from whence thou comest?

RAPHAEL

O Adam, one Almighty is, from whom
All things proceed, and up to Him return.
All display various forms, various degrees
Of substance, and, in things that live, of life.
Time may come when men
With angels may participate, and find
That from these corporal nutriments, perhaps,
Your bodies may at last turn all to spirit,
Improved by tract of time, and, winged, ascend
Ethereal as we, or may at choice
Here or in Heavenly paradises dwell.
If ye be found obedient, and retain
Unalterably firm His love entire
Whose progeny you are.

ADAM

What meant that caution joined, 'If ye be found
Obedient'? Can we want obedience then
To him, or possibly His love desert,
Who formed us from the dust, and placed us here
Full to the utmost measure of what bliss
Human desires can seek or apprehend?

RAPHAEL

Son of Heaven and Earth,
Attend. That thou art happy, owe to God.
That thou continuest such, owe to thy self,
That is, to thy obedience.
This was that caution given thee, be advised.
God made thee perfect, not immutable.
And good He made thee, but to persevere
He left it in thy power, ordained thy will
By nature free, not over-ruled by fate.

Our voluntary service He requires,
Not our necessitated.
Myself and all the angelic host that stand
In sight of God enthroned, our happy state
Hold, as you yours, while our obedience holds,
On other surety none. Freely we serve
Because we freely love, as in our will
To love or not. In this we stand or fall.
And some are fallen, to disobedience fallen,
And so from Heaven to deepest Hell. O fall!
From what high state of bliss into what woe!

ADAM

Attentive, and with more delighted ear,
Divine instructor, I hear. We knew not
To be both will and deed created free.
Yet that we never shall forget to love
Our Maker and obey Him whose command
Single, is yet so just. Though what thou tellst
Hath passed in Heaven, some doubt within me moves
But more desire to hear, if thou consent,
The full relation, which must needs be strange,
Worthy of sacred silence to be heard.

RAPHAEL

High matter thou injoinst, O prime of men,
Sad task and hard, for how shall I relate
To human sense the invisible exploits
Of warring spirits? How last unfold
The secrets of another world, perhaps
Not lawful to reveal? Yet for thy good
This is dispensed. There came a day in Heaven
On which the Father Infinite begot
His only Son, appointing him the head

Of all his host, his right hand, our own lord.
All seemed well pleased with this, but all were not.
Satan, so call him now, his former name
Is heard no more in Heaven, he was then fraught
With envy 'gainst the Son of God, that day
Deep malice didst conceive and high disdain.
With lies he led his legions, who made up
One third of all the host, intending to
Erect a throne equal to God's, throughout
The spacious north. At length they came
Upon a mountain, where Satan, seeming
To claim equality with the High Lord,
Set down his royal seat. God saw them go
And, resolving to put down this Godless crew,
Sent forth his armed saints invincible
Led by Gabriel and myself, to battle
With military prowess and defeat.
Now storming fury rose with horrid shock
And clamour such as heard in Heaven 'til now
Was never. Arms on armour clashing brayed
Horrible discord, and the madding wheels
Of brazen chariots rang. Dire was the noise
Of conflict. For two days full war was raged.
First Satan and his legions climbing high
And nearly touching victory, then we,
The holy army of the Lord, drawing
Them back, with the power of faithfulness,
Didst overwhelm them quite and God sent forth
His Son, with war and thunder, to pursue
These loathsome spirits and drive them out beyond
All Heaven's bounds down into the utter deep.
The Messiah came with twenty thousand saints
Blazing aloft and, in final battle,
Astonished Satan and his rebellious crew,

Driving them before His thunderous wrath
Unto the wall of Heaven which, opening wide,
Rolled inward and the wasteful void disclosed.
The sight struck them back affeard, but far worse
Urged them behind. Headlong themselves they threw
Down from the verge of Heaven. Nine days they fell,
'Til Hell at last, the house of woe and pain,
Yawning received those dreadful legions whole
And on them closed. All Heaven sang triumphant
For the only victor and his holy Father.
At thy request and that thou mayst beware
By what has passed, to thee I thus reveal
The discord which befell, and war in Heaven
Among the angelic powers, and the deep fall
Of those too high aspiring, who rebelled
With Satan, he who envies now thy state,
Who now is plotting how he may seduce
Thee also from obedience.
But listen not to his temptations, warn
Thy Eve and let it profit thee to have heard
By terrible example the reward
Of disobedience. Firm they might have stood,
Yet fell. Remember and fear to transgress.

Exit RAPHAEL.

ADAM

O Eve! Associate sole!
Now doubts possess me, for hearest thou
What hath been warned us, what malicious foe
Envying our happiness, and of his own
Despairing, seeks to work us woe and shame
By sly assault, and somewhere nigh at hand
Watches, no doubt, with greedy hope to find

His wish and best advantage.
Pray, leave not the faithful side
That gave thee being, lest tempting harms
Befall thee severed from me.

EVE

That such an enemy we have, I know.
But that thou shouldst my firmness therefore doubt
To God and thee, because we have a foe
May tempt it, I expected not to hear.
If his fraud is thy fear, that plain infers
Thy equal fear that my firm faith and love
Can, by his fraud, be shaken or seduced.

ADAM

Daughter of God and Man, for such thou art,
And as such, free from sin and blame entire,
Not diffident of thee do I dissuade
Thy absence from my sight, but to avoid
The attempt itself, intended by our foe.
Subtle must be he who seduced angels.
I, from the influence of thy looks, receive
Access in every virtue, in thy sight
More wise, more watchful, stronger, if need were
Of outward strength.
Why shouldst not thou like sense within thee feel
When I am present, and thy trial choose
With me best witness of thy virtue?

EVE

If this be our condition, thus to dwell
In narrow circuit straightened by a foe,
Subtle or violent,
How are we happy, still in fear of harm?

For harm precedes not sin. His foul esteem
Sticks no dishonour on our front, but turns
Foul on himself, so wherefore shunned or feared
By us?
Let us not suspect our happy state,
Left so imperfect by the Maker wise,
As not secure to single or combined.
Frail is our happiness if this be so
And Eden were no Eden thus exposed.

ADAM

O Woman, best are all things as the will
Of God ordained them, His creating hand
Nothing imperfect or deficient left.
If thou think trial unsought may find
Us both secure, thus warned I let thee go.
Go in thy native innocence, rely
On what thou hast of virtue, summon all,
For God towards thee hath done His part, do thine.

EVE

With thy permission then and thus forewarned
The willinger I go, nor much expect
A foe so proud will first the weaker seek,
So bent, the more shall shame him his repulse.

> *Exit EVE and ADAM separately. THE SON reveals
> the Tree of Knowledge, and hanging upon it, an apple.
> Enter SATAN, who slowly approaches...*

Act Four

THE FALL

SATAN

O Earth, how like to Heaven, if not preferred
More justly, seat worthier of gods, as built
With second thoughts, reforming what was old!
For what god, after better, worse would build?
With what delight could I have walked thee round,
If I could joy in aught. Sweet interchange
Of hill and valley, rivers, woods and plains,
Now land, now sea and shores with forest crowned,
Rocks, dens and caves, but I in none of these
Find place or refuge, and the more I see
Pleasures about me, so much more I feel
Torment within me. All good to me becomes
Bane, and in Heaven much worse would be my state.
But neither here seek I, no, nor in Heaven
To dwell,
For only in destroying I find ease
To my relentless thoughts.
Thus wrapped in mist
Of midnight must I glide obscure and pry
In every bush and brake, where hap may find
The serpent sleeping, in whose mazy folds
To hide me and the dark intent I bring.
O foul descent! That I who erst contended
With gods to sit the highest, am now constrained
Into a beast and mixed with bestial slime.
But what will not ambition and revenge
Descend to? Who aspires must down as low
As high he soared, obnoxious first or last

To basest things. Revenge, at first though sweet,
Bitter, ere long, back on itself recoils.
Let it. I reck not, so it light well aimed,
Since higher I fall short, on him who next
Provokes my envy, this new favourite
Of Heaven, this man of clay, son of despite,
Whom us the more to spite, his Maker raised
From dust. Spite he with spite is best repaid!

SATAN becomes a snake. Enter EVE.

Let me not let pass
Occasion which now smiles. Behold alone
The woman, opportune to all attempts.
Her husband, for I view far round, not nigh.
She fair, divinely fair, fit love for gods.

He approaches her.

Wonder not, Sovereign Mistress, if perhaps
Thou canst, who art sole wonder, much less arm
Thy looks, the heaven of mildness, with disdain,
Displeased that I approach thee thus and gaze
Insatiate.
Fairest resemblance of thy Maker fair,
Thee all things living gaze on, all things thine
By gift, and thy celestial beauty adore.
In this enclosure wild, these beasts among,
Beholders rude and shallow to discern
Half what in thee is fair, one man except,
Who sees thee (and what is one?), who shouldst be seen
A goddess among gods, adored and served
By angels numberless, thy daily train.

EVE

What may this mean? Language of man pronounced
By tongue of brute and human sense expressed?
The first at least of these I had thought denied
To beasts, whom God on their creation day
Created mute to all articulate sound.
Thee, serpent, subtlest beast of all the field,
I knew, but not with human voice endued.
Redouble then this miracle and say
How camest thou speakable of mute, and how
To me so friendly grown above the rest
Of brutal kind that daily are in sight?

SATAN

Empress of this fair world, resplendent Eve,
Easy to me it is to tell thee all
What thou commandst and right thou shouldst be obeyed.
I was at first as other beasts that graze
The trodden herb, of abject thoughts and low,
'Til on a day roaving the field, I chanced
A goodly tree far distant to behold
Loaden with fruit of fairest colours mixed,
Ruddy and gold. I nearer drew to gaze.
To satisfy the sharp desire I had
Of tasting those fair apples, I resolved
Not to defer. Hunger and thirst at once,
Powerful persuaders, quickened at the scent
Of that alluring fruit, urged me so keen.
About the mossy trunk I wound me soon,
For high from ground the branches would require
Thy utmost reach or Adam's.
Amid the tree now got, where plenty hung
Tempting so nigh, to pluck and eat my fill
I spared not, for such pleasure 'til that hour

At feed or fountain never had I found.
Sated at length, ere long I might perceive
Strange alteration in me, to degree
Of reason in my inward powers, and speech.
Thenceforth to speculations high or deep
I turned my thoughts, and with capacious mind
Considered all things visible in Heaven,
Or Earth, or Middle, all things fair and good.
But all that fair and good in thy divine
Semblance, and in thy beauty's heavenly ray,
United, I beheld no fair to thine
Equivalent or second, which compelled
Me thus, though importune perhaps, to come
And gaze, and worship thee of right declared
Sovereign of Creatures, Universal Dame.

EVE

Serpent, thy overpraising leaves in doubt
The virtue of that fruit, in thee first proved.
But say, where grows the tree, from hence how far?
For many are the trees of God that grow
In Paradise, and various, yet unknown
To us.

SATAN

Empress, the way is ready, and not long.
If thou accept
My conduct, I can bring thee thither soon.

EVE

Lead then.

They approach the tree.

Serpent, we might have spared our coming hither,
Fruitless to me, though fruit be here to excess,
For of this tree we may not taste nor touch.
God so commanded, and left that command
Sole daughter of His voice. The rest, we live
Law to ourselves, our reason is our law.

SATAN

Indeed? Hath God then said that of the fruit
Of all these garden trees ye shall not eat,
Yet lords declared of all in Earth or air?

EVE

Of the fruit
Of each tree in the garden we may eat,
But of the fruit of this fair tree amidst
The garden, God hath said, 'Ye shall not eat
Thereof, nor shall ye touch it, least ye die.'

SATAN

Queen of this universe, do not believe
Those rigid threats of death; ye shall not die!
How should ye? By the fruit? It gives you life
To knowledge. By the threatener, look on me,
Me who have both touched and tasted and yet live.
Shall that be shut to Man, which to the beast
Is open? Or will God incense His ire
For such a petty trespass, and not praise
Rather your dauntless virtue,
Deterred not from achieving what might lead
To happier life, knowledge of good and evil.
Of good, how just? Of evil, if what is evil
Be real, why not known, since easier shunned?

God therefore cannot hurt ye, and be just.
Not just, not God.
Why then was this forbid? Why but to awe,
Why but to keep ye low and ignorant,
His worshippers. He knows that in the day
Ye eat thereof, your eyes that seem so clear,
Yet are but dim, shall perfectly be then
Opened and cleared and ye shall be as gods,
Knowing both good and evil as they know.
And what are gods that Man may not become
As they, participating god-like food?
If they all things are, then who enclosed
Knowledge of good and evil in this tree,
That whoso eats thereof, forthwith attains
Wisdom without their leave? And wherein lies
The offence, that Man should thus attain to know?
What can your knowledge hurt Him, or this tree
Impart against His will, if all be His?
Or is it envy, and can envy dwell
In heavenly breasts? These, these and many more
Causes import your need of this fair fruit.
Goddess human, reach then, and freely taste.

EVE

Great are thy virtues, doubtless, best of fruits.
Whose taste, too long forborn, at first assay
Gave elocution to the mute, and taught
The tongue not made for speech to speak thy praise.
Thy praise He also who forbids thy use
Conceals not from us, naming thee the Tree
Of Knowledge, knowledge both of good and evil;
Forbids us then to taste, but His forbidding
Commends thee more, while it infers the good
By thee communicated, and our want.

In plain then, what forbids He but to know,
Forbids us good, forbids us to be wise?
Such prohibitions bind not. But if death
Bind us with after-bands, what profits then
Our inward freedom? In the day we eat
Of this fair fruit, our doom is, we shall die.
How dies the Serpent? He hath eaten and lives,
And knows, and speaks, and reasons, and discerns,
Irrational 'til then. For us alone
Was death invented? Or to us denied
This intellectual food, for beasts reserved?
What fear I then, rather what know to fear
Under this ignorance of good and evil,
Of God or death, of law or penalty?
Here grows the cure of all, this fruit divine,
Fair to the eye, inviting to the taste,
Of virtue to make wise. What hinders me
To reach, and feed at once both body and mind?

*She picks off an apple and bites. Silence. When she
looks around, SATAN has disappeared. She bites
again. Enter ADAM.*

Hast thou not wondered, Adam, at my stay?
Thee I have missed, and thought it long, deprived
Thy presence, agony of love 'til now
Not felt, nor shall be twice, for never more
Mean I to try, what rash, untried, I sought,
The pain of absence from thy sight. But strange
Hath been the cause, and wonderful to hear.
This tree is not, as we are told, a tree
Of danger tasted, nor to evil unknown
Opening the way, but of divine effect
To open eyes, and make them gods who taste.

It hath been tasted such: the serpent wise,
Or not restrained as we, or not obeying,
Hath eaten of the fruit, and is become,
Not dead, as we are threatened, but thenceforth
Endued with human voice and human sense,
Reasoning to admiration, and with me
Persuasively hath so prevailed, that I
Have also tasted, and have also found
The effects to correspond. Opener mine eyes
Dim erst, dilated spirits, ampler heart,
And growing up to godhead, which for thee
Chiefly I sought, without thee can despise.
Thou therefore also taste, that equal lot
May join us, equal joy, as equal love.

ADAM

How art thou lost? How on a sudden lost?
Defaced, deflowered, and now to death devoted?
Rather, how hast thou yielded to transgress
The strict forbiddance, how to violate
The sacred fruit forbidden! Some cursed fraud
Of enemy hath beguiled thee, yet unknown!
But past who can recall, or done undo?
Not God omnipotent, nor Fate, yet so
Perhaps thou shalt not die. Perhaps the fact
Is not so heinous now, foretasted fruit,
Profaned first by the serpent, by him first
Made common and unhallowed ere our taste.
Nor yet on him found deadly, he yet lives,
Lives, as thou saidst, and gains to live as man
Higher degree of life, inducement strong
To us, as likely tasting to attain
Proportional ascent, which cannot be
But to be gods, or angels, demi-gods.

Nor can I think that God, Creator wise,
Though threatening, will in earnest so destroy
Us His prime Creatures.
So now with thee I hereby fix my lot.
How can I live without thee, how forgo
Thy sweet converse and love so dearly joined,
To live again in these wild woods forlorn?
Should God create another Eve, and I
Another rib afford, yet loss of thee
Would never from my heart. No, no! I feel
The link of nature draw me. Flesh of flesh,
Bone of my bone thou art, and from thy state
Mine never shall be parted, bliss or woe.

EVE

Were it I thought death menaced would ensue
This my attempt, I would sustain alone
The worst and not persuade thee, rather die
Deserted, than oblige thee. But I feel
Far otherwise the event, not death, but life
Augmented.
On my experience, Adam, freely taste
And fear of death deliver to the winds!

*ADAM takes the apple and bites. The lights change.
THE SON moves forwards.*

THE SON

They plucked. They ate,
And all the world trembled from her entrails.
Earth felt the wound and nature from her seat,
Sighing through all her works, gave signs of woe
That all was lost.
The sky lowered and, muttering thunder, sad drops

Wept at completing of the mortal sin
Original. For all was lost.

ADAM

Eve, now I see thou art exact of taste.
Much pleasure we have lost, while we abstained
From this delightful fruit, nor known 'til now
True relish, tasting. If such pleasure be
In things to us forbidden, it might be wished
For this one tree had been forbidden ten.
But come, so well refreshed, now let us play,
As meet is, after such delicious fare.
For never did thy beauty, since the day
I saw thee first and wedded thee, adorned
With all perfections, so enflame my sense
With ardour to enjoy thee, fairer now
Than ever, bounty of this virtuous tree.

They kiss. Suddenly ADAM pulls away.

O Eve! In evil hour thou didst give ear
To that false worm, of whomsoever taught
To counterfeit man's voice, true in our fall,
False in our promised rising. Since our eyes
Opened we find indeed, and find we know
Both good and evil, good lost, and evil got.
Bad fruit of knowledge, if this be to know,
Which leaves us naked thus, of honour void,
Of innocence, of faith, of purity!
How shall I behold the face
Henceforth of God or angel, erst with joy
And rapture oft beheld? O might I here
In solitude live savage, in some glade
Obscured, where highest woods impenetrable,

To star or sun-light, spread their umbrage broad,
And brown as evening. Cover me you pines
And cedars, with innumerable boughs
Hide me, where I may never see them more.
Would thou hadst harkened to my words, and stayed
With me, as I besought thee, when that strange
Desire of wandering this unhappy morn,
I know not whence possessed thee. We had then
Remained still happy, not as now, despoiled
Of all our good, shamed, naked, miserable.

EVE

What words have passed thy lips, Adam severe?
Imput'st thou that to my default, or will
Of wandering, as thou callst it, which who knows
But might as ill have happened thou being by,
Or to thy self perhaps, hadst thou been there.
Was I to have never parted from thy side?
As good have grown there still a liveless rib.
Being as I am, why didst not thou the head
Command me absolutely not to go,
Going into such danger as thou saidst?
Thou didst permit, approve, and fair dismiss.
Hadst thou been firm and fixed in thy dissent,
Neither had I transgressed, nor thou with me.

ADAM

Is this the love, is this the recompence
Of mine to thee, ungrateful Eve, expressed
Immutable when thou wert lost, not I,
Who might have lived and joined immortal bliss,
Yet willingly chose rather death with thee.
And am I now upbraided, as the cause

Of thy transgressing? Not enough severe,
It seems, in thy restraint. What could I more?
I warned thee, I admonished thee, foretold
The danger, and the lurking enemy
That lay in wait. Beyond this had been force,
And force upon free will hath here no place.
But confidence then bore thee on, secure
Either to meet no danger, or to find
Matter of glorious trial. And perhaps
I also erred in overmuch admiring
What seemed in thee so perfect, that I thought
No evil durst attempt thee, but I rue
That error now, which is become my crime,
And thou the accuser.

GABRIEL enters. ADAM and EVE hide.

GABRIEL

Where art thou Adam, wont with joy to meet
My coming seen far off? I miss thee here.

They come forward.

ADAM

I heard thee in the Garden, and of thy voice
Afraid, being naked, hid myself.

GABRIEL

My voice thou oft hast heard, and hast not feared,
But still rejoiced, how is it now become
So dreadful to thee? That thou art naked, who
Hath told thee? Hast thou eaten of the tree
Whereof God gave thee charge thou shouldst not eat?

ADAM

O Heaven! In evil straight this day I stand
Before my judge, either to undergo
Myself the total crime, or to accuse
My other self, the partner of my life,
Whose failing I should conceal, not expose.
I see that I should hold my peace, yet thou
Wouldst easily detect what I conceal.
This woman whom God made to be my help,
And gave me as His perfect gift, so good,
That from her hand I could suspect no ill,
She gave me of the tree, and I did eat.

GABRIEL

Was she thy god, that her thou didst obey
Before His voice? Or was she made thy guide,
Superior, or but equal, that to her
Thou didst resign thy manhood?

Silence.

Say, woman, what is this which thou hast done?

EVE

The serpent me beguiled, and I did eat.

Silence.

GABRIEL

Then on the Serpent thus my curse let fall.
Because thou hast done this, thou art accursed
Above all cattle, each beast of the field.
Upon thy belly grovelling thou shalt go,

And dust shalt eat all the days of thy life.
   (*To EVE.*)
Thy sorrow I will greatly multiply
By thy conception. Children thou shalt bring
In sorrow forth, in pain and agony.
   (*To ADAM.*)
Because thou hast hearkened to the voice of thy wife,
And eaten of the tree which was forbid,
Cursed is the ground for thy sake, thou in sorrow
Shalt eat thereof all the days of thy life.
Thorns also and thistles it shall bring thee forth
Unbid, and thou shalt eat the herb of the field.
In the sweat of thy face shalt thou eat bread,
'Til thou return unto the ground, for thou
Out of the ground wast taken, know thy birth,
For dust thou art, and shalt to dust return.
God thinks not much to clothe his enemies,
Father and mother of thy family,
Hide thy nakedness.

> *He hands them clothes which they put on.*
> *Exit GABRIEL.*

ADAM

O miserable of happy! Is this the end
Of this new glorious world, and me so late
The glory of that glory, who now become
Accursed of blessed, hide me from the face
Of God, whom to behold was then my height
Of happiness.
Who of all ages to succeed, but feeling
The evil on him brought by me, will curse
My head, and rue their ancestor impure,
With, 'For this we may thank Adam.' O fleeting joys

Of Paradise, dear bought with lasting woes!
Did I request Thee, Maker, from my clay
To mould me Man, did I solicit Thee
From darkness to promote me, or here place
In this delicious Garden?
Be it so. This doom is fair.

*ADAM and EVE pray. Suddenly SIN and DEATH,
led by SATAN, crash through the walls of Eden.*

SATAN

Fair daughter, and thou son and grandchild both,
High proof ye now have been given as the race
Of Satan (for I glory in the name,
Antagonist of Heaven's almighty King)!
Man by fraud I have seduced
From his Creator, and, the more to increase
Your wonder, with an apple!
See I have tempted and brought low mankind
For the infernal empire.
Here dwell and reign in bliss, hence on the Earth
Dominion exercise and in the air.
Chiefly on Man, sole lord of all declared,
Him first make sure your thrall, and lastly kill.
My substitutes I send ye.
On your joint vigour now
My hold of this new kingdom all depends,
Through Sin to Death, exposed by my exploit.
If your joint power prevails, the affairs of Hell
No detriment need fear, go and be strong.

DEATH

To me, who with eternal famine pine,
Alike is Hell, or Paradise, or Heaven,

There best, where most with ravin I may meet,
Which here, though plenteous, all too little seems
To stuff this maw, this vast unhide-bound corpse.

SATAN

Thou on these herbs, and fruits, and flowers
Feed first, on each beast next, and fish, and fowl,
No homely morsels, and whatever thing
The sithe of time mows down, devour unspared.

SIN

'Til I in Man residing through the race,
His thoughts, his looks, words, actions all infect,
And season him thy last and sweetest prey.

*The three move off into the trees. After a moment,
THE SON follows. ADAM and EVE raise their
heads.*

ADAM

I submit!
That dust I am, and shall to dust return!
O welcome hour whenever. Why delays
Thy hand to execute what Thy decree
Fixed on this day? Why do we overlive?
Why are we mocked with death, and lengthened out
To deathless pain? Thus what I now desire,
And what I fear, alike destroys all hope
Of refuge, and concludes me miserable
Beyond all past example and future.
O Conscience, into what abyss of fears
And horrors hast thou driven me, out of which
I find no way, from deep to deeper plunged!

Enter GABRIEL and RAPHAEL with flaming swords.

RAPHAEL

Adam, Heaven's high behest no preface needs.
Sufficient that thy prayers are heard, and death,
Then due by sentence when thou didst transgress,
Defeated of his seizure many days are
Given thee of grace, wherein thou mayst repent,
And one bad act with many deeds well done
Mayst cover.

GABRIEL

Well may then thy Lord appeased
Redeem thee quite from death's rapacious claim.
But longer in this Paradise to dwell
Permits not. To remove thee we are come,
And send thee from the Garden forth to till
The ground whence thou wast taken, fitter soil.

EVE

O unexpected stroke, worse than of death!
Must we thus leave thee Paradise? Thus leave
Thee native soil, these happy walks and shades,
Fit haunt of gods? Where I had hope to spend,
Quiet though sad, the respite of that day
That must be mortal to us both. From flowers,
How shall I part, and whither wander down
Into a lower world, to this obscure
And wild, how shall we breathe in other air
Less pure, accustomed to immortal fruits?

RAPHAEL

Lament not Eve, but patiently resign
What justly thou hast lost; nor set thy heart,
Thus over-fond, on that which is not thine.
Thy going is not lonely, with thee goes
Thy husband, him to follow thou art bound.
Where he abides, think there thy native soil.

GABRIEL

Come, follow.
The Arch-Angel moved and high in front advanced.
The brandished sword of God before them blazed
Fierce as a comet and with torrid heat.

THE SON

In either hand the hastening angel led
Our lingering parents to the Eastern gate
Of Paradise, so late their happy seat.

ADAM

They, looking back, all the Eastern side beheld
Of Paradise, so late their happy seat,
Waved over by that flaming brand, the gate
With dreadful faces thronged and fiery arms.

EVE

Some natural tears they dropped, but wiped them soon.
The world was all before them, where to choose
Their place of rest and providence their guide.
They hand in hand with wandering steps and slow,
Through Eden took their solitary way.

They reach the back wall and an enormous door opens. ADAM and EVE move through into darkness and it closes behind them. The angels exit.

Silence.

SATAN enters, followed by THE SON. He stands for a moment in the empty space, and then slowly moves off.

Lights dim on THE SON, alone...

Epilogue

Father, Thy word is past and Man thus falls.
From now, all aid and grace mankind
Can never seek, so dead in sins and lost.
Attonement for himself or offering meet,
Indebted and undone, hath none to bring.
Behold me then. Me for him. Life for life.
On me let Death wreck all his rage.
On me let Thine anger fall.

He unwraps the bandages on his hands, revealing
bloody wounds.

Yet that debt paid,
Thou wilt not leave me in the loathsome grave
His prey, nor suffer my unspotted soul
Forever with corruption there to dwell,
But I will rise, subduing my vanquisher.
I'll lead Hell captive, meagre Hell, and show
The powers of darkness bound,
And with the multitude of my redeemed,
I'll enter Heaven long absent, and return
To see Thy face.
Wrath shall be no more thenceforth,
But in Thy presence joy entire.
For Man's sake I will leave Thy bosom
And for him I'll freely die.
Account me man.

Lights rise as he extends his arms into the crucifix.
Blackout.

ALSO AVAILABLE FROM OBERON BOOKS

DERREK HINES
GILGAMESH

Set in ancient Iraq, *Gilgamesh* is the story of a despotic king, a wild man and their battle with the vengeance of the gods. In this electrifying adaptation, the poet Derrek Hines reinvents his acclaimed version of this ancient epic for the 21st century stage, complete with hand grenades, mobile phones and fun-fair rides.

'Not so much a translation as a vibrant and vigorous reimagining of the world's first book, which should take its place alongside Heaney's Beowulf *and Hughes's* Ovid*'*
The New Statesman

ISBN 1 84002 654 5 • £8.99

www.oberonbooks.com

SULAYMAN AL-BASSAM
THE MIRROR FOR PRINCES

Set in Iraq c. 750 AD, at the dawn of the Abbasid revolution, the poet, wit and radical reformer Ibn Al-Muqaffa is battling against fervent revolutionaries, heretic poets, religious propagandists, and a ruler who names himself none other than 'God's shadow on earth'.

Part history, part political fable, part personal tragedy, this new drama explores the creation of one of the masterpieces of Eastern literature, *Kalila wa Dimna* or *The Mirror for Princes*, through the life of its most important scribe.

ISBN 1 84002 670 7 • £8.99

www.oberonbooks.com

KNEEHIGH THEATRE
TRISTAN & YSEULT
WITH
THE BACCHAE • THE WOODEN FROCK • THE RED SHOES

Tristan & Yseult is one of Britain's oldest love stories brought vividly to life by one of Britain's most exciting theatre companies. Published alongside three of their other adaptations, this is the definitive performance-text for Kneehigh Theatre's five-star production, performed to sell-out audiences at the National Theatre and throughout the country.

'*It made me want to gurgle with delight... I loved it with a passion.*' The Guardian

'*High, heroic passion. I found myself successively gripped, touched and moved.*' The Times

'*One of the best evenings in theatre you could hope to find.*' The Independent

ISBN 1 84002 564 6 • £9.99

www.oberonbooks.com

PETER OSWALD
THE RAMAYANA

In Peter Oswald's acclaimed adaptation of this ancient Hindu epic, the divine incarnation Rama sets out on a journey to set his wife Sita free from the demon Ravana. A keystone of religious mythology, *The Ramayana* is about the rise of humanity from animal to god.

ISBN 1 84002 201 9 • £7.99

For information on these and other plays and books published by Oberon, or for a free catalogue, listing all titles and cast breakdowns, visit our website

www.oberonbooks.com

info@oberonbooks.com • 020 7607 3637